018

SO-ART-855

Roadrunner

by Eloise Macgregor

Consultants:

Judy Liddell
Director, Audubon New Mexico

Kimberly Brenneman, PhD
National Institute for Early Education Research, Rutgers University, New Brunswick, New Jersey

BEARPORT PUBLISHING

New York, New York

Credits

Cover, Sekar B/Shutterstock; 2, © Bierchen/Shutterstock; 4, © Florian Andronache/Shutterstock; 5, © John Cancalosi/Alamy; 7, © Jim David/Shutterstock; 8, © Dennis W. Donohue/Shutterstock; 9, © Ron Sanford Photography/iStock; 10, © iStock; 11, © ZUMA Press, Inc./Alamy; 12, © John Cancalosi/Alamy; 13TL, © Ryan M. Bolton/Shutterstock; 13TR, © Vibe Images/Shutterstock; 13CL, © Gallinago_media/Shutterstock; 13C, © CreativeNature.nl/Shutterstock; 13BL, © Jessica Kuras/Shutterstock; 13BR, © William Silver/Shutterstock; 14TL, © B & T Media Group Inc./Shutterstock; 14TR, © Eric Isselee/Shutterstock; 14BL, © Peggy Sells/Shutterstock; 14BR, © Eric Isselee/Shutterstock; 15, © Warren Price Photography/Shutterstock; 16, © Tim Pleasant/Angel DiBilio/Shutterstock; 17, © gracious_tiger/Shutterstock; 18, © the4js/Shutterstock; 19, © Doris Evans; 20, © Doris Evans; 21, © Doris Evans; 22L, © azuswebworks/Shutterstock; 22R, © Jason Mintzer/Shutterstock; 23TL, © Tim Pleasant/Angel DiBilio/Shutterstock; 23TM, © Videowokart; 23TR, © Sasha Buzko/Shutterstock; 23BL, © gracious_tiger/Shutterstock; 23BM, © CreativeNature.nl/Shutterstock; 23BR, © mlorenz/Shutterstock.

Publisher: Kenn Goin
Creative Director: Spencer Brinker
Design: Alix Wood
Editor: Jessica Rudolph
Photo Researcher: Alix Wood

Library of Congress Cataloging-in-Publication Data

Macgregor, Eloise, author.
  Roadrunner / by Eloise Macgregor.
     pages cm.—(Desert animals : searchin' for shade)
  Includes bibliographical references and index.
  ISBN 978-1-62724-533-3 (library binding)—ISBN 1-62724-533-2 (library binding)
  1. Roadrunner—Juvenile literature. 2. Desert animals—Juvenile literature. I. Title.
  QL696.C83M32 2015
  598.7'4—dc23
                                        2014036714

For more information, write to Bearport Publishing Company, Inc., 45 West 21st Street, Suite 3B, New York, New York 10010. Printed in the United States of America.

10 9 8 7 6 5 4 3 2 1

Contents

Meet a Roadrunner

It's a hot summer day in the **desert**.

A roadrunner speeds across the rocky ground.

The bird is chasing a cricket.

The insect tries to hop away, but the bird is too fast.

The roadrunner catches the cricket and gobbles it up.

roadrunner

Roadrunners are often seen running along roads and paths. That's how they got their name.

cricket

A Desert Home

Roadrunners live mostly in the deserts of North America and Central America.

Some live on **grasslands** or on the edges of woods.

Very little rain falls in deserts and grasslands.

Only a few plants can grow in the dry soil, such as cactuses and sagebrushes.

There are two kinds of roadrunners. The greater roadrunner is the larger of the two. It measures around 22 inches (56 cm) long from the tip of its beak to the end of its tail. The lesser roadrunner is around 16 inches (41 cm) long.

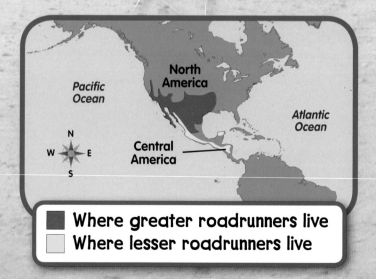

Pacific Ocean

North America

Atlantic Ocean

N
W   E
S

Central America

■ Where greater roadrunners live
☐ Where lesser roadrunners live

In the desert, it can be very hot during the day and cold at night.

To stay cool during the day, a roadrunner rests in the shade under some plants.

To stay warm at night, it fluffs up its feathers to trap warm air.

Then, in the early morning, the bird sits out in the sun.

After warming up in the sun, the roadrunner is ready to go hunting.

a roadrunner resting in the shade of a cactus

8

a roadrunner warming up in the sun

In summer, desert temperatures sometimes reach 120°F (49°C) during the day. On a winter's night, the temperature can drop to below freezing.

Do you think roadrunners are better at running or flying?

Fly or Run?

Most birds are better at flying than running but not roadrunners.

Roadrunners can only fly short distances.

Their wings are too small to lift their bodies off the ground for long.

However, roadrunners have strong legs that help them run fast.

Their long tails keep their bodies balanced when they run.

Of the birds that can both run and fly, roadrunners are the fastest runners. They can run up to 17 miles (27 km) per hour. Ostriches can run faster, but they cannot fly.

long tail

small wings

Do you think roadrunners hunt for food by running, flying, or both?

Roadrunners can outrun most **prey**.

The birds hunt animals such as lizards, snakes, and mice.

To kill a mouse or other small animal, a roadrunner jabs it with its sharp beak.

To kill a large rattlesnake, the bird first pecks the snake's head.

Then the roadrunner grabs the snake by the tail.

The bird slams the rattlesnake's head against the ground until the animal is dead.

rattlesnake

Roadrunner Foods

scorpion

rattlesnake

small bird

field mouse

lizard

grasshopper

Roadrunners also hunt by flying or jumping and catching insects or birds in midair.

How do you think roadrunners stay safe from enemies?

Roadrunners are fast, but they still have to watch out for **predators**.

Animals such as hawks, bobcats, and some kinds of snakes hunt roadrunners or eat their eggs.

When a roadrunner spots a predator, it runs away as quickly as it can.

Then the bird hides among plants until the predator moves on.

Roadrunner Enemies

hawk

rat snake

raccoon

bobcat

A roadrunner makes a clicking sound when it spots predators. The sound is a warning to other roadrunners that danger is nearby.

Male and female roadrunners find **mates** in spring or fall.

To **attract** a female, a male roadrunner makes a loud "cooing" noise.

Then he dances for the female!

The male also uses his beak to offer food to the female.

If the female takes the food, the birds become mates and start to build a nest.

a male roadrunner offering a female some food

Where do you think roadrunners build their nests?

a female roadrunner

Roadrunners usually keep the same mates for their entire lives.

a male roadrunner dancing

Making a Nest

A male and a female roadrunner build their nest in a plant.

The male brings twigs and other materials to the female.

She makes the nest a few feet above the ground.

She lines it with soft grasses, feathers, roots, or snakeskin.

Then, over the next three days, the female lays between three to five eggs.

After about 20 days, chicks hatch from the eggs.

a male roadrunner collecting twigs

Sometimes, if a male roadrunner is taking too long collecting sticks to build the nest, the female will call out to him.

a roadrunner mother taking care of chicks that have hatched

roadrunner chicks

eggs

A Roadrunner Family

The roadrunner chicks grow quickly.

By the time they are three weeks old, the young birds start to run and catch small prey.

When they are one or two months old, they leave their parents' nest.

They speed off into the desert to start their own adult lives.

As the chicks grow, the parents sometimes make the sides of the nest taller so the babies don't fall out.

a young roadrunner practicing running

young roadrunners

Science Lab

Be a Roadrunner Scientist

Imagine you are a scientist who studies roadrunners.

Write a report to tell other people all about how roadrunners live in their desert homes.

Use information in this book to help you.

Draw pictures to include in your report.

When you are finished, present your report to your friends and family.

Here are some words you can use when writing or talking about roadrunners.

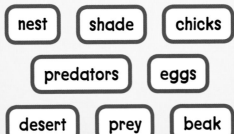

nest shade chicks

predators eggs

desert prey beak

Read the questions below and think about the answers.

You can include some of the information from your answers in your report.

- *Why do roadrunners rest in the middle of the day?*

- *How do roadrunners kill their prey?*

- *What animals hunt roadrunners?*

- *How does running help roadrunners survive?*

Science Words

attract (uh-TRAKT) to cause an animal to like or be interested in something

desert (DEZ-urt) dry land with little rainfall and few plants

grasslands (GRASS-landz) dry places with lots of grasses; few trees and bushes grow there

mates (MAYTS) male or female partners

predators (PRED-uh-turz) animals that hunt and eat other animals

prey (PRAY) animals that are hunted and eaten by other animals

Index

Read More

Borgert-Spaniol, Megan. *Roadrunners (Blastoff! Readers)* Minneapolis, MN: Bellwether Media (2014).

Macken, JoAnn Early. *Roadrunners.* Milwaukee, WI: Weekly Reader Early Learning (2006).

Schaefer, Lola M. *Roadrunners (Heinemann Read and Learn).* Chicago, IL: Heinemann Library (2004).

Learn More Online

To learn more about roadrunners, visit **www.bearportpublishing.com/DesertAnimals**

About the Author

Eloise Macgregor lives in Cornwall, England. She writes nonfiction books for children, mostly about wildlife. She keeps pet chickens, and her favorite wild animals are sloths.